The Vikings
AND ALL THAT

For Caitlin and Emma

The Vikings
AND ALL THAT

Allan Burnett

Illustrated by
Scoular Anderson

First published in 2016 by
Birlinn Limited
West Newington House
10 Newington Road
Edinburgh
EH9 1QS

www.bcbooksforkids.co.uk

ISBN: 978 1 78027 393 8

British Library Cataloguing-in-Publication Data
A catalogue record for this book is available from the British Library

Designed by James Hutcheson

Page make up by Mark Blackadder

Printed and bound by Grafica Veneta SpA
(www.graficaveneta.com)

Contents

Prologue   7

1 The Viking age   13
2 Boats and battle-axes   19
3 The Viking empire   31
4 How to be a Viking   45
5 Viking explorers   59
6 The Viking universe   71
7 The curse of the horned helmet   81

Timeline   93

Prologue

Storm clouds gathered overhead as a fleet of mighty ships appeared on the horizon. The vessels surged menacingly towards the shore with their large, square sails bulging in the wind.

At the water's edge, farmers from a local village looked on in terror. Christian monks from the nearby monastery prayed to heaven. Then they all turned and ran for it.

The first ship beached on the shingle with a crash, while lightning flashed in the sky. Hordes of men from the ships leapt into the shallows to chase after the fleeing villagers as the rain pelted down.

One local lad was too slow. He felt the collar of his tunic being grabbed by a muscular hand.

'Please don't kill me!' squealed the boy as he turned around and dropped to his knees.

'Kill you?' said the invader, surprised. 'No, I just want to do business with you.'

'Eh?' said the boy, who was now confused as well as terrified.

'We come in peace to trade and make friends,' continued the invader. 'I hate it when people just run away like that.'

'B-B-But . . . y-y-you're a Viking!' exclaimed the boy. 'Everyone knows you Vikings plunder and pillage wherever you go!'

'Don't judge a book by its cover, my lad,' said the Viking, who had a bushy, red beard.

The Viking began setting up a stall and laying out some trinkets.

The boy could not believe his eyes and ears. He had always been told that the Vikings were ruthless barbarians who liked nothing better than to go berserk and then tear people limb from limb.

But this lot were not violent Viking raiders – they were peaceful Viking *traders*.

As the rain clouds disappeared and sunlight began to stream down, the boy stumbled along the beach. He found more Viking stalls selling everything from pots of honey to animal furs and statues carved from walrus tusks.

Some of the Vikings had sat down to play board games. Still others were cooking up tasty treats like roast horse-meat and nettle soup.

Slowly, the villagers and holy men began to return. After a while they were all laughing and joking with the newcomers, and the Vikings did a roaring trade.

Just then, the distant blast of a horn could be heard. The outline of new ships appeared on the distant waves. These vessels had dragons carved on their bows and looked a lot more frightening than the last lot.

From the sides of each craft protruded rows of many oars. They were being thrust back and forth in time with loud chanting and drumming.

'Right lads, time to make way!' commanded the red-bearded Viking.

Suddenly the stalls were packed up and the board games snapped shut. The traders hastened back to their boats and began pushing and heaving them into the water.

'Wait!' shouted the boy, running into the shallows and pointing at the approaching ships. 'Who's *that*?'

'Oh, they're Viking *raiders*,' came the breathless reply from Red Beard. 'Ruthless barbarians who tear people limb from limb. The leader is called Bjorn Bonecrusher.'

'Why Bonecrusher?' asked the boy.

'You'll find out soon enough!' shouted Red Beard as he leapt back into his boat. 'Anyway, got to go. Have a nice day!'

The boy sheepishly watched the peaceful Vikings hastily sailing away just as the arriving warships bore down on the beach. He turned to the people behind him . . .

When the raiders hit the shore the outcome was every bit as horrible as you might imagine. These Vikings were indeed vile and violent.

The locals were lashed and the monks were mauled. Bjorn Bonecrusher did a lot of bone-crushing that day.

But don't get too upset. If you are worried about what happened to the boy, don't be. He didn't actually exist in real life. And nor did his attackers.

Well, not exactly.

The dramatic scene you have just read is intended to explain a key Viking fact, which is this: when *real* Vikings turned up, some came in peace while others came to kill. Although usually not at the same time!

If fascinating and frightening facts float your boat, then you'll be pleased to know that the rest of this book is packed with the stuff.

Warning: from here on in, the mayhem is for real.

That means lots of grisly and gruesome details about Viking raiders, their weapons and their favourite methods of making people-flavoured mincemeat.

On the other hand, the pages that follow also have a lot to say about the other kind of Viking – the peaceful kind. That's because there was much more to the Vikings than just raiding and robbery.

By reading on you will discover who the Vikings really were. You will learn about the strange things they ate and the crazy clothes they wore. You'll get to know their loopy languages and their bizarre beliefs. And you'll find out where they went, as well as what they got up to when they arrived.

So first things first: let's find out where the Vikings came from and how their story begins . . .

1

The Viking age

The Vikings lived about a thousand years ago. That's roughly from the eighth century through to the twelfth century. These centuries are known as 'the Viking age'.

During that time, the Vikings invaded and conquered many lands. They built an empire of sorts that stretched all the way from North America to Russia.

The Vikings had a big impact on the British Isles. They ruled over parts of England, Scotland and Ireland for a long time.

There'll be more about all that in the chapters to come. In the meantime, let's begin by looking at the homeland of the Vikings and how they got their name.

The Vikings originally came from Scandinavia. This is a region of northern Europe whose countries include Denmark, Norway and Sweden.

Scandinavia is a land of forests, fields and lakes. These days it is a very modern place. In many ways, though, it has not changed much since Viking times.

Some parts of Scandinavia are low and flat, others are lofty and mountainous. In winter it is often extremely cold, especially in the north where there is hardly any light at all.

In summer, it can be very warm and the daylight never-ending.

Some houses are far inland but most people live near the sea, just as they did during Viking times. Others live on small islands, of which there are many, dotted around the Scandinavian coasts.

One island that was popular with the Vikings is Gotland. It lies in the Baltic Sea to the east of mainland Sweden. Modern archaeologists have dug up many Viking treasures there, including thousands of silver coins.

Scandinavia is also home to many wild animals such as elk, wolves, bears and poisonous snakes – just as it was during the Viking age. The Vikings liked to carve pictures of such wild beasts on their jewellery and weapons.

Wild animals are still occasionally hunted in Scandinavia just as they were in Viking times, and other animals such as cows and sheep are farmed just as they were then.

Viking farms and villages had large byres for sheltering their cattle from bad weather. There were also great halls made of turf and timber, where Viking chiefs held court. The grandest halls were built for kings and queens.

Some famous Viking royals included:

King Harald Finehair. Born around 860 AD, Harald made a promise not to cut or comb his hair until he became king of all Norway. He was nicknamed 'Shaggyhair' until he eventually became king and got a haircut.

Queen Thyra. She lived in the early 900s and was the wife of Gorm the Old, one of the first kings of Denmark. According to legend, Thyra built a wall to protect the Danes from German invaders.

King Harald Bluetooth. King of Denmark and Norway, Harald was the son of Thyra and Gorm. He erected a huge standing stone in his parents' honour at a place called Jelling. The stone was carved with runes – the Vikings' ancient written language.

Many Vikings lived in towns. These were places where lots of people could come together to buy and sell everything from barley for making porridge to whetstones used for sharpening blades and tools.

Over time the farmers, merchants and craftsmen of Viking villages and towns prospered. There was more and more food to eat, houses became better and children could grow up to be stronger and healthier.

All that sounds rather good. Except that the Vikings are famous for abandoning Scandinavia in search of new lands. So here's a question: what made them decide to leave?

Here's an answer: nobody knows for sure.

Some historians believe that the population of Scandinavia eventually became too big. This might sound strange when you consider that Scandinavia is a very big place, and that during Viking times most of it had no inhabitants at all. Surely there was more than enough room for everybody?

The trouble was that only a small part of the land was good for farming. This meant that there was not enough good land or food to go around. So some people had to find a new place to live.

Others say that the reason people left Scandinavia was because of their royals and chieftains. These leaders had a taste for the good life and they demanded that Viking traders and raiders sail overseas to bring back treasure.

As time went on, many Vikings reckoned that owning land was more valuable than owning jewels or coins. So the Vikings set their sights on conquering other countries.

Bringing back treasure or gaining new land was sometimes accomplished peacefully by trade. This meant selling things to the locals in return for goodies to take away in a boat, or a piece of territory to settle on.

On other occasions, of course, the Vikings used force. In other words they sailed off to slaughter people, steal their stuff and seize their soil.

Some historians point out that the Vikings were especially keen on looting churches and killing Christians. We'll come back to that later.

In the meantime, let's talk about the meaning of the word 'Viking'. Many historians believe that people in Scandinavia did not actually call themselves Vikings *unless* they were setting out on a peaceful trade trip or a violent raid.

If you were sailing off to do a bit of trading or raiding, then you were 'going on a viking' – as in going on a voyage, or going on a shopping trip. The people who went on a viking included men, women and sometimes even children.

Over time, these people came to be known simply as Vikings, especially in places they raided such as England, where Viking was another word for 'robber' or 'pirate'.

Before we investigate the places where the Vikings went raiding, let's take a closer look at the equipment they needed in order to 'go on a viking'. Among the most important items were ships and weapons . . .

2

Boats and battle-axes

The Vikings are famous for their ships. They are also well known for their skull-splitting swords and axes, but we'll come to those in a minute.

One reason why the Vikings became such keen boat-builders is simply that Scandinavia is a really big place. People often lived far apart from one another and they needed a handy way to keep in touch.

But surely it was easier to travel over land on foot, or on horseback?

Well, that was certainly true in some places. But remember, much of Scandinavia is boggy forest and steep mountains. Travelling for long distances over land could be a real chore, not to mention dangerous with all those bears and wolves roaming the place.

I told you we should have gone by boat!

So for many people during the Viking age, it was actually much easier to get around by boat. This gave people all the more reason to build their villages and towns near the sea or by a river.

Of course, the boats needed to be well built if Vikings were to cross the sea between Denmark and Sweden, or sail up the fjords and rivers of Norway. For a start, it was important to have all the right building materials.

Luckily, all that forestry gave the Vikings plenty of timber.

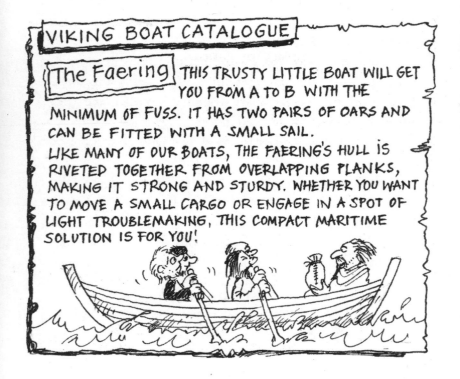

VIKING BOAT CATALOGUE

The Faering THIS TRUSTY LITTLE BOAT WILL GET YOU FROM A TO B WITH THE MINIMUM OF FUSS. IT HAS TWO PAIRS OF OARS AND CAN BE FITTED WITH A SMALL SAIL.
LIKE MANY OF OUR BOATS, THE FAERING'S HULL IS RIVETED TOGETHER FROM OVERLAPPING PLANKS, MAKING IT STRONG AND STURDY. WHETHER YOU WANT TO MOVE A SMALL CARGO OR ENGAGE IN A SPOT OF LIGHT TROUBLEMAKING, THIS COMPACT MARITIME SOLUTION IS FOR YOU!

A big, old oak was the ideal tree for making a boat. The tree trunk was split apart by a team of people working with axes. They then sliced it up to make planks for the ships' hulls.

The rivets that fastened the planks and other bits and pieces together were made from iron, while the sails were made from wool.

Viking ships came in many different shapes and sizes, and were designed for different types of voyage. So a Viking had to choose carefully.

The Longship

DESIGNED FOR MAXIMUM IMPACT, THIS BOAT IS THE ULTIMATE SEA GOING WAR MACHINE. IT'S BIG, FAST AND LONG. WITH THIRTY PAIRS OF OARS UNDER ITS LARGE, SQUARE SAIL, THE LONGSHIP WILL GET YOUR WARRIORS TO THEIR NEXT RAIDING DESTINATION IN NO TIME.

UNIQUE, SHALLOW-DRAFT TECHNOLOGY MEANS SHIP CAN BE SAILED IN WATER ONE METRE DEEP!

VERY LIGHT – CAN BE PICKED UP BY THE CREW AND HAULED OVERLAND – NO VILLAGE IS SAFE!

Besides using their boats for trading and raiding, the Vikings also used them for fishing and hunting. One of the most valuable things the Vikings hunted for at sea was walrus tusk, otherwise known as walrus ivory. This ivory was turned into a range of precious objects we'll look at later on.

For now, the main thing to remember is that Vikings really loved boats. In fact, they loved boats so much they engraved pictures of boats on their coins – and sometimes were even buried with them.

Vikings were also buried with their weapons. It was a way of showing off that you had been a great warrior in life. Favourite Viking weapons included:

THE BATTLE-AXE THIS WAS THE VIKINGS' MOST POPULAR WEAPON. IT WAS USED IN DIFFERENT WAYS.

1 THROWING SMALL, LIGHT AXES COULD BE THROWN BY SPINNING THEM IN THE AIR. THIS TOOK PRACTICE!

2 | SWINGING | AN AXE COULD BE SWUNG AT YOUR ENEMY AT CLOSE QUARTERS. THE LONG-HANDLED, BROAD AXE WAS GOOD FOR THIS.

3 | CHOPPING | THE BEARDED AXE HAD A BLADE THAT HUNG DOWN LIKE A BEARD. GOOD FOR CHOPPING WOOD -AND CHOPPING OFF HEADS, TOO!

| SPEARS AND JAVELINS | CHEAP AND SIMPLE WEAPONS WITH SMALL METAL BLADES AT THE END OF A WOODEN SHAFT. LONG SPEAR GOOD FOR THRUSTING, JAVELIN GOOD FOR THROWING.

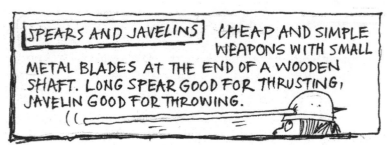

BOWS AND ARROWS

VIKINGS USED LONGBOWS FOR FIGHTING AS WELL AS HUNTING. THE BOW WAS MADE OF STRONG YET FLEXIBLE YEW WOOD. IT COULD BE TWO METRES LONG. ARROWHEADS WERE MADE OF IRON.

A SWORD

A SWORD WAS THE GRANDEST WEAPON A VIKING COULD OWN. CHEAP ONES WERE MADE OF IRON - THE FINEST, MOST EXPENSIVE BLADES USED POLISHED STEEL. THE HILT (HANDLE) COULD BE DECORATED WITH SILVER OR GOLD.

Of course, getting your hands on the right weapons was only half the battle. A Viking warrior also needed the right clothes and armour.

We don't know exactly what armour and clothes the Vikings wore, but the look was something like this:

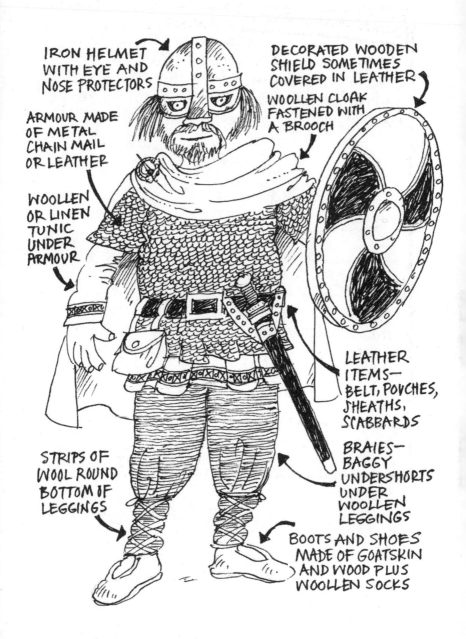

IRON HELMET WITH EYE AND NOSE PROTECTORS

DECORATED WOODEN SHIELD SOMETIMES COVERED IN LEATHER

ARMOUR MADE OF METAL CHAIN MAIL OR LEATHER

WOOLLEN CLOAK FASTENED WITH A BROOCH

WOOLLEN OR LINEN TUNIC UNDER ARMOUR

LEATHER ITEMS— BELT, POUCHES, SHEATHS, SCABBARDS

STRIPS OF WOOL ROUND BOTTOM OF LEGGINGS

BRAIES— BAGGY UNDERSHORTS UNDER WOOLLEN LEGGINGS

BOOTS AND SHOES MADE OF GOATSKIN AND WOOD PLUS WOOLLEN SOCKS

VIKING WOMEN — THEY WORE LONG DRESSES OF LINEN OR WOOL.

CAPE HELD BY A BROOCH

HEADSCARF

DECORATIVE APRON HELD BY BROOCHES

As soon as some Viking warriors put all their fighting gear on, some legends say they went *berserk*. That is, they would fly into a fit of murderous rage.

Perhaps a Viking would go berserk because *braies* and leggings took so long to untie when he needed a wee that he ended up wetting himself? Well, maybe.

But according to Viking legend, there was a more serious reason. If a warrior went berserk he would become super-human. He could not be stopped by a blade and could run through fire.

Wearing the skin of a wolf or a bear, a *berserker* would bite his shield and run at the enemy in a fury, killing anyone who got in his path with one blow!

Berserker legends should be taken with a pinch of salt. Nobody knows how many Vikings actually went berserk, or what powers they really had. Some historians think Vikings went berserk because they ate mind-altering mushrooms or drank way too much alcohol. (A favourite Viking drink was mead, made from honey.) Berserkers also attacked warriors on their own side, which made them a bit of a nuisance.

One thing is for sure, though. When Viking warriors got tooled up with weapons and boarded their longships, they were not setting off on a sightseeing cruise.

They were usually out to storm distant shores, steal treasures and slay anyone who got in their way – as the people of Britain and Ireland soon found out . . .

3

The Viking empire

When the Vikings left home they made their mark on many different lands, and none more so than Britain and Ireland, where they built a kind of empire.

In the year 789 AD, three Viking ships beached at Wessex on the south coast of England. A local official rode out to greet them. The details of what happened next are very sketchy. But it might have gone something like this . . .

The leader of the Vikings, who did not understand the local language very well, shrugged.

The official dismounted his horse and tried again, speaking slow and clear. 'Who . . . are . . . you?'

A short Viking behind the leader piped up. 'Northmen!'

'Ahh,' said the official. 'You must be from Denmark.'

The Vikings looked at each other. There was more shrugging.

'Norway?' tried the official again.

The Viking leader stared back impatiently. His men started to fidget with their weapons.

'Look, it doesn't matter,' said the official, raising his hands in a calming gesture. 'Now, what may I ask is your business here?'

The short Viking whispered something in his leader's ear.

'Trade,' said the leader gruffly.

'Excellent!' The official clapped his hands together. 'I'll just have to take you back to the royal court in Dorchester so we can get you registered.'

'No, trade now!' repeated the Viking leader angrily.

'Errr . . . I'm afraid I can't do that. You see, we have certain *rules . . .*'

The official came to a dead stop as a Viking sword was plunged into his belly. He dropped to his knees, gave a last gasp and slumped face down in the sand.

'No rules!' shouted the Viking leader. The others roared in agreement.

The Vikings got back in their boats and sailed away. But if you thought they were an impatient and violent bunch, just wait until you hear about the next lot.

In 793 AD more Viking warships set sail for Northumbria in north-east England. Apparently the locals knew something was up because terrible omens were later reported by a medieval history book called the Anglo-Saxon Chronicle.

Sure enough, on 8 June that year the Vikings arrived. They beached their shallow-bottomed longboats on the Holy Island of Lindisfarne just off the Northumbrian coast.

Lindisfarne was home to a monastery – a village where Christian monks worked and prayed. A holy man called Cuthbert was buried there. It was, all in all, a very sacred place.

But not to the Vikings. They poured out of the boats and thundered up the beach looking for any treasures they could lay their hands on.

✺ INSTRUCTION MANUAL ✺ FOR RAIDING A MONASTERY

1 LAND AND HEAD FOR THE CHURCH. THIS IS WHERE THE CHRISTIAN TREASURES ARE.

2 REMOVE ALL VALUABLES: GOLD CHALICES, SILVER PLATES, CRUCIFIXES, SILK ROBES, JEWEL-ENCRUSTED BOOKS. IF IT WON'T BUDGE - VANDALISE IT.

3 KILL ANYONE WHO GETS IN YOUR WAY. VIKINGS ARE PAGANS - CHRISTIAN MONKS HATE US - GIVE IT TO 'EM HOT!

4 SPEAKING OF HOT, MAKE SURE TO BURN THE HOUSES AND CHURCH. GRAB ANYTHING YOU FANCY - FOOD, ANIMALS, SLAVES, WHATEVER.

5 DON'T HANG ABOUT IN CASE REINFORCEMENTS TURN UP. LOAD UP, HEAD FOR HOME (AND FEASTING).

6 ANYONE TRYING TO STOP YOU? DROWN THEM ON THE WAY OUT.

7 THROW A FEW SPEARS AT ANYONE STILL ALIVE ON SHORE. THEY WILL TELL STORIES ABOUT HOW **AWESOMELY TERRIFYING** WE VIKINGS ARE. JOB DONE.

After Lindisfarne, the Vikings paid a visit to many more monasteries, including:

Jarrow – Also in Northumbria, Jarrow was hit in 794. But the locals fought back and killed the Viking leader. As the other Vikings fled, a storm wrecked their ships.
Iona – This Scottish island monastery was attacked at least three times, in 795, 802 and 806. On the third occasion, the Vikings went truly berserk and massacred sixty-eight monks while looting the place. A famous Christian book called the Book of Kells had to be

moved from Iona to Ireland for safekeeping.

Rathlin – Lying between Ireland and Scotland, this was another island monastery. It was plundered by Norwegian nutcases in 795.

After a few decades it seems the Vikings' behaviour towards the Brits and Irish changed. Instead of quick in-and-out raids, the Vikings started staying for longer. This seems to be because they became less interested in stealing treasure and more interested in conquering land.

The Vikings set about conquering parts of mainland Scotland around the early 800s, wreaking havoc among the local Celtic population. But some Vikings might have settled on Scottish islands such as Orkney and Shetland much earlier than that.

The Vikings then began settling in Ireland. In 841 they built a fortress at Dublin. It was ruled for a long while by a Viking called Olaf the White and it became a popular place to do business. Among the things traded in Dublin were:

Decorated weapons
Exotic silk fabrics from Asia
Human slaves.

Other Irish cities originally built by the Vikings include Cork, Limerick, Waterford and Wexford. Since the Vikings made such a big impression on Ireland, the natives had a special name for them – which was *Gaill*.

Gaill means foreigners. To the Celtic people of Ireland (and Scotland) the Vikings certainly were foreigners – and often very hostile ones at that.

For example, Olaf the White of Dublin attacked Scotland on more than one occasion. In 870 he and another Viking called Ivar the Boneless laid siege to the mighty fortress at Dumbarton Rock on the River Clyde.

The Celtic inhabitants of the castle defended it from the invaders until the Vikings cut off their water supply. Then the Vikings burst in, looted the place and took many locals as slaves.

But over time, many Vikings in Ireland and Scotland stopped being foreigners. They settled down, got married to locals, made local friends (and enemies, naturally) and became part of the native populations.

Meanwhile, back in England, things were a bit different.

England had once been a Celtic country but was now a patchwork of Anglo-Saxon kingdoms. The Vikings built a powerful kingdom of their own here, but they never really shook off their reputation as foreigners and outsiders.

The Viking conquest of England goes something like this. First, there was a bit of a false start. In 851, a huge fleet of dragon-headed Viking ships sailed up the River Thames. They raided London and the southeast. But they were slaughtered in battle in Wessex, at the same time as another Viking fleet was defeated in a great sea battle off Kent.

The Vikings were not the type to give up easily. In 866 a great army from Denmark invaded Northumbria and captured the town of York – or 'Jorvik', as the Vikings liked to call it.

Then, in 869, the Vikings had a go at East Anglia. They killed the king, Edmund, and chopped off his head. But just when it looked like the Vikings might conquer the whole of England, the natives fought back.

After a few setbacks, Alfred, the King of Wessex, thumped the invaders in 878. Then in 886 he forced the Viking king, Guthrum, to sign a peace treaty.

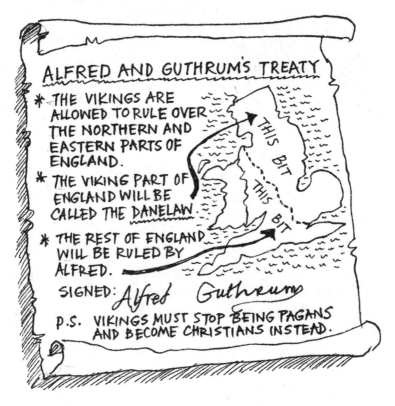

ALFRED AND GUTHRUM'S TREATY

* THE VIKINGS ARE ALLOWED TO RULE OVER THE NORTHERN AND EASTERN PARTS OF ENGLAND.

* THE VIKING PART OF ENGLAND WILL BE CALLED THE DANELAW.

* THE REST OF ENGLAND WILL BE RULED BY ALFRED.

SIGNED: Alfred Guthrum

P.S. VIKINGS MUST STOP BEING PAGANS AND BECOME CHRISTIANS INSTEAD.

THIS BIT

THIS BIT

It was a good deal. No wonder Alfred became known as 'Alfred the Great'. Things didn't stay peaceful for too long, though.

The Anglo-Saxons – in other words the English – were keen to take the Danelaw back.

KNUT'S SON,
HAROLD HAREFOOT,
RULES FOR 5 YEARS.

THEN HIS BROTHER,
HARTHAKNUT, RULES
FOR 2 YEARS.
HE TAXES THE ENGLISH
UNFAIRLY AND
THEY REBEL.
A REBEL LANDOWNER
CALLED LADY GODIVA
IS SAID TO HAVE
PROTESTED AGAINST
HARTHAKNUT BY
RIDING NAKED
THROUGH THE
STREETS OF COVENTRY.

IN 1042, HARTHAKNUT
DIES SUSPICIOUSLY
WHILE DRINKING
AT A WEDDING PARTY.

GHURGH!

THE VIKINGS HAD ANOTHER GO BUT THEIR
LEADER, HARALD HARDRADA WAS HAMMERED
BY THE ANGLO-SAXONS AT THE BATTLE OF
STAMFORD BRIDGE IN 1066

Just days after the Battle of Stamford Bridge, a new bunch of invaders called the Normans arrived from France and took over England. The Vikings were well and truly finished.

These events made 1066 rather an important year in English history. So important it has a book named after it – *1066 and All That*.

So much for England. But what about Wales?

Well, the Vikings often raided Wales but never got much more than a foothold. In the 856, a tough Celtic king called Rhodri Mawr battered an invading Viking fleet at the Welsh island of Anglesey. Rhodri killed the Viking leader, who was called Gorm.

Later on, in the early eleventh century, another Viking army harassing Wales was kept at bay by being paid off with silver. This was an example of Viking blackmail – more about that in the next chapter.

Meanwhile over in Ireland, Viking power eventually crumbled. At the Battle of Clontarf in 1014 they were clobbered at the hands of an army led by Celtic King Brian Boru.

Brian died during the battle but was remembered as an Irish hero. Those Vikings who were not killed or driven away settled down peacefully and became Irish.

It was really only in Scotland and the Isle of Man that the Vikings hung around for a *seriously* long time. The Norwegian Vikings who settled on Man held an open-air parliament to discuss important matters. This was based on the parliament back in Norway and was called a *thing*.

When Viking warriors died on Man, some were buried along with their weapons and even their horses and dogs. Not only that but their girlfriends too. These girls – who were probably slaves – had the tops of their heads sliced off!

The Norwegians didn't lose their grip on Man until 1266 when they agreed to sell it to the Scottish King Alexander III. The Vikings also handed over the Hebrides, where they had ruled the roost for generations.

As usual with the Vikings, getting rid of them had not been peaceful. In 1263, Haakon IV, the Viking ruler of Norway, had sailed through the Hebrides and attacked mainland Scotland at Largs in the Firth of Clyde.

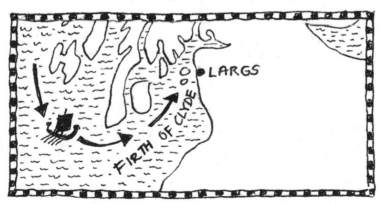

But Haakon's ships lost control in a storm. When they hit the shore, Alexander III's men skewered, slashed and sliced them up on the beach until the sea ran red with their blood. Haakon got away, but died later while recovering up in Orkney.

Speaking of Orkney, these islands, along with Shetland, remained under Viking rule right up until 1468. Even today, these Northern Isles of Scotland remain very 'Viking' in all sorts of ways.

We'll take a closer look at that later. For now, it's time to discover how YOU can live like a Viking . . .

4

How to be a Viking

Viking life was often exciting and fun. So much fun, in fact, that you might be tempted to give it a try yourself. But if you want to live like a Viking, there are a few things you need to learn.

Luckily you already know a lot. For example, you have discovered what the word 'Viking' means. It's any person from Scandinavia who lived around a thousand years ago and went off on a boat for a bit of raiding or trading.

But there's more.

Take Viking habits, for example. You already know the Vikings had an exceedingly bad habit of bashing anybody who got in their way.

Other bad Viking habits included scribbling graffiti, hoarding stuff, taking hostages, blackmailing people and going berserk!

So let's start with graffiti. Have you ever scribbled something you shouldn't have, somewhere you shouldn't have?

Well, the Vikings did that too. On the wall of an ancient burial chamber called Maes Howe in Orkney, a Viking bragged, 'These runes were carved by the best rune-carver.'

Another one wrote,

Speaking of which, the Vikings loved hoarding treasure: gold, silver, weapons, jewels . . . you name it.

Archaeologists are still finding Viking hoards today. Some people use metal detectors to locate treasure buried under gardens, fields and beaches. If you're lucky you might dig some up yourself.

Most of us don't have heaps of gold to hoard, though. Instead we often hoard things we don't need, such as toys we no longer play with, or shoes we don't wear any more. That's definitely a bad habit.

Sometimes it was tricky for Viking raiders to lay their hands on treasure. So they stole people.

People were kidnapped and taken hostage on Viking ships until a ransom was paid. If the Vikings were satisfied with the ransom – which might be paid in coins or weapons – then the hostages would be returned safe and well.

But if the Vikings didn't get what they were after, the hostages might be taken as slaves and sold off in distant lands.

Taking hostages was a form of blackmail. The basic idea of blackmail is that you need to pay someone to stop them doing something bad.

Another kind of blackmail the Vikings liked was when people paid to be left alone and not raided. If the natives didn't pay up, they could expect to be burned and butchered.

The Anglo-Saxons of England, for example, paid blackmail to the Vikings to be left alone. This payment was known as the *Danegeld*.

When it came to burning, butchering and robbing, let's not forget about the *berserkers*. Like most Viking bad habits, going berserk is one that's probably best avoided.

So much for bad habits. But you might also be wondering whether the Vikings had any *good* habits you could take up. You know – peaceful hobbies like art, sports and games.

Well, the Vikings did enjoy these pastimes, but many of them were not exactly peaceful. And some were exceedingly dumb and dangerous. Take these games for example:

STUPID SWIMMING

TWO OPPONENTS JUMP INTO A LAKE. EACH ONE HAS TO TRY AND HOLD THE OTHER UNDER WATER UNTIL THEY GIVE UP - OR DROWN.

WRETCHED WRESTLING

A POPULAR STYLE OF WRESTLING WAS GLIMA. TO WIN A WRESTLING MATCH, A VIKING WOULD OFTEN LIFT HIS OPPONENT OFF THE GROUND AND SMASH HIM OVER A STONE.

WHAGH!

BRAINLESS BALL·GAME

THE GAME OF KNATTLEJKR WAS PLAYED BY TWO TEAMS WITH A BALL AND STICKS. IT WAS VERY VIOLENT AND VERY LONG, WITH MATCHES LASTING A WHOLE DAY.

WHUMP!

CRACK!

Most of these gruesome games ought to be avoided. Luckily, though, there are some more sensible options available, such as:

BRAINY BOARD GAMES

THE VIKINGS PLAYED CHESS AND BACKGAMMON. THEY ALSO HAD A GAME CALLED TEFL IN WHICH A KING HAS TO ESCAPE FROM THE BOARD WITHOUT BEING CAPTURED.

The boards and playing pieces in Viking games were often beautifully crafted. This tells us a lot about another thing that was important to the Vikings – art and design.

You already know about the Vikings' finely decorated weapons and ships. But they also made beautiful statues and figurines, elaborate woodcarvings and awesome picture stones.

A famous group of picture stones is on the Swedish island of Gotland. Chiselled into one rock is a kind of cartoon strip in which a warrior leaves the battlefield and makes the journey up to Valhalla – Viking heaven.

Hard materials like stone, wood and metal were not the only things with which the Vikings made art. Soft fabrics and textiles such as wool and silk were popular too.

Tapestries, for example, were made from woven cloth onto which animals, people and other scenes were stitched. These tapestries could be hung on a wall or buried in someone's grave along with other treasures.

Speaking of cloth and fabric, we have already looked at Viking clothes. So let's take a closer look at how the Vikings used their arts and crafts skills to really dress up.

If a Viking man or woman wanted to impress, they could add the following items to their outfit:

THE VIKING CATALOGUE

STYLISH BROOCH FOR KEEPING CLOAK OR DRESS IN PLACE.

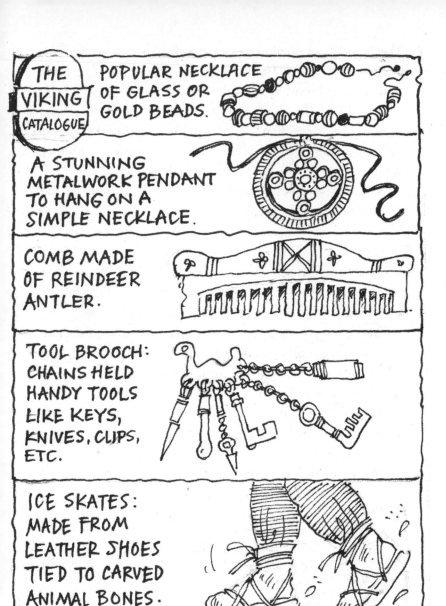

THE VIKING CATALOGUE

POPULAR NECKLACE OF GLASS OR GOLD BEADS.

A STUNNING METALWORK PENDANT TO HANG ON A SIMPLE NECKLACE.

COMB MADE OF REINDEER ANTLER.

TOOL BROOCH: CHAINS HELD HANDY TOOLS LIKE KEYS, KNIVES, CLIPS, ETC.

ICE SKATES: MADE FROM LEATHER SHOES TIED TO CARVED ANIMAL BONES. PRACTICE REQUIRED!

THE VIKING CATALOGUE

HORSE: A DEPENDABLE BEAST FOR RIDING AND FARMING. NAILS WERE HAMMERED INTO THEIR HOOVES TO KEEP THEM STEADY ON WINTER ICE. HORSES WERE ALSO EATEN.

If you haven't got nails in your hooves your'e probably dinner!

Speaking of horsemeat, there was one area of life that had a huge range of accessories and tools all of its own – Viking food and drink.

Archaeologists have discovered all sorts of Viking accessories for making and eating food and drink. These include farming tools and millstones for grinding flour. Then there are pots, jugs, decorated drinking horns and lots more besides.

Bowls, cups and plates were often made of wood. Spoons could also be made of wood or sometimes bone.

So we have a good idea of what the Vikings used to farm their food and serve it to their family and friends. But what exactly did they eat? (Apart from horsemeat!)

Well, the Vikings also kept cattle, sheep, goats and pigs. These beasts gave them milk, meat and fat (as well as wool, bone and leather).

The Vikings also scoured the rivers, lakes and seas for fish. And they hunted more exotic creatures, such as:

Elk, deer, wild boar and bears from the forests and mountains.
Whales and walrus from the icy northern seas.

In fields near their villages they grew crops such as barley, wheat and rye. They also grew or gathered vegetables and fruits.

Throw all these things together and you have all the meals a Viking family needed to get through the day:

Breakfast – A typical first meal of the day might have been meat and vegetable stew with a hunk of bread, washed down with some milk.
Lunch – The Vikings generally had no time for lunch-breaks. But they might pull a cloth package out of their pouch and tuck into a bit of cheese and bread while on the go.

Dinner – More stew and perhaps a bit of salted fish. Fresh apples and berries would be eaten when in season, and a drink of ale or mead – the strong stuff made from honey – was always popular.

The Viking 'kitchen' was primitive. The most important thing in it was the cauldron – a huge pot that was hung over a fireplace, or hearth. In the cauldron, stews and other meals were cooked.

The hearth was the heart of the home. The rest of a typical Viking house had space for people to sleep and go about their daily business.

Unlike the grand fortresses and halls where chiefs and royals lived, a normal Viking family lived in a much more basic house.

The way these houses were built depended on what building materials were available. They might be made of stone, wood or turf – which is blocks of grassy earth cut out of the ground.

Here's an example:

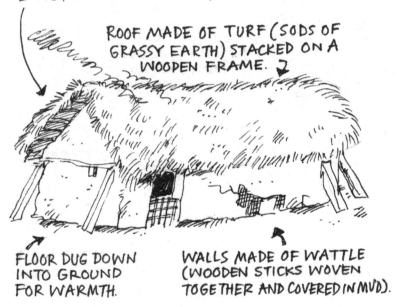

LONG, BOX-LIKE SHAPE, OFTEN JUST ONE ROOM.

ROOF MADE OF TURF (SODS OF GRASSY EARTH) STACKED ON A WOODEN FRAME.

FLOOR DUG DOWN INTO GROUND FOR WARMTH.

WALLS MADE OF WATTLE (WOODEN STICKS WOVEN TOGETHER AND COVERED IN MUD).

Beds were arranged next to the walls and were often really basic – a flat bench with a mattress made from heather, straw or feathers.

The type of house you lived in – as well as your job – had a lot to do with your place in Viking society. Viking society was a bit like an imaginary pyramid. This is roughly how it worked:

King – at the very top of society, this royal ruler lived with his queen and family in the biggest and best houses, halls and fortresses. Below the king were the . . .

Jarls – The rich chiefs. They owned a lot of land and ran trading businesses. They also lived in grand houses and lorded it over their own workers and other members of society, such as the . . .

Karls – The normal people. They lived in the type of house we've just been looking at. Karls did all sorts of jobs such as farming and making things. The main thing is that they were free, unlike . . .

Thralls – The lowest of the low, they were slaves owned by someone higher up the social pyramid. A lucky thrall could be freed by a kind master, or even find enough money to buy his or her freedom.

By now you should be getting a good idea of how to live like a Viking. But don't forget you also need a Viking nickname.

Erik 'Bloodaxe' is one of those we have already encountered. If you think that sounds scary, how about Thorfinn 'Skull-Splitter'? He was a Viking from Orkney and judging by the name must have been pretty nasty.

Viking nicknames weren't always scary, though. Sometimes they were just daft. One of Skull-Splitter's grandsons was known as 'Buttered-Bread' and another was called 'Hard-Mouth'.

Why not come up with your own Viking nickname? Something like:

Sarah Snot-Sneezer
Chris Crazy-Hair
Marwan Mint-Muncher

Of course, having a nifty nickname, a homely house and some well-crafted treasures was all very good. But there was something else a Viking needed if he or she really wanted to show off: fancy foreign goods. Things like wine, art, weapons . . . you name it, so long as it was foreign and exclusive.

Of course, we've already learned a lot about Viking trade in the British Isles. But more fabulous goods came from even further afield.

To find out what these things were and where they came from, let's follow the Viking explorers . . .

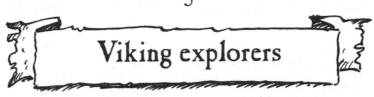

5

Viking explorers

Exploring is something the Vikings were really good at. They spread their sails and travelled to distant, foreign lands in search of many things, such as treasure, land and slaves.

They travelled around Scandinavia, of course, and to the British Isles and Ireland. But the Vikings did an awful lot more exploring than that.

This meant they encountered all sorts of fascinating folk. Take the Sami people of far northern Scandinavia, for example.

The Sami were, and many still are, reindeer herders and fishermen. Their homeland is a mountainous place above the Arctic Circle called Sápmi (the proper name for Lapland).

The Sami traded with many Vikings, including a famous explorer called Ohthere.

Oh, there you are, Ohthere!

Ohthere collected many valuable items from the Sami, which he could sell in faraway places such as Denmark or England. Such Sami goods included:

Whale bones (carved into cutlery or jewellery).
Bird feathers (turned into quill pens or fishing floats).
Reindeer skins (for coats, boots and bedding).
Ships' cables (ropes made from seal skin).

While on his travels, Ohthere was keen to find out how far north the land stretched. This meant a voyage lasting many weeks and covering thousands of miles.

Ohthere sailed up the coast to the very tip of Norway.

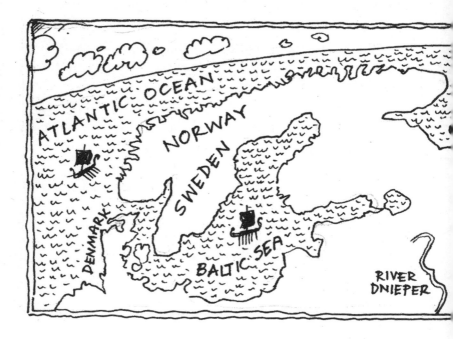

He then continued eastwards round the northern edge of Scandinavia all the way to Russia. But he dared not hang around in case he was attacked!

There was a much easier way for the Vikings to reach Russia. They sailed from the south of Scandinavia across the Baltic Sea, which was often nice and warm during the summer.

It was the Swedish Vikings who tended to sail east to Russia (while Danish and Norwegian Vikings tended to go west).

To explore Russia, the Vikings sailed along three big rivers – the Don, the Dnieper and the Volga. And can you take a wild guess as to what the Vikings got up to when they made landfall?

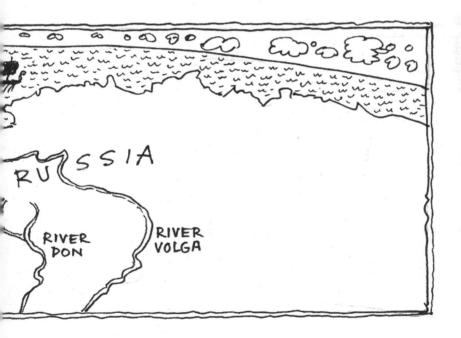

A. Trading
B. Raiding
C. Blackmailing
D. Conquering
E. All of the above

You guessed it, the answer is **E** – a bit of everything. In fact some Vikings settled down in Russia while others ventured as far south and east as the Black Sea and the Caspian Sea.

Vikings even popped up in Byzantium (which nowadays is part of Turkey) as well as Arabia and Egypt. From these distant lands, goodies such as exotic seashells were transported all the way back to Scandinavia.

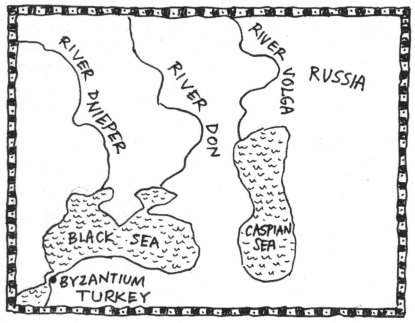

But hold on a minute. Does all this mean that the most intrepid and adventurous Vikings were those who went east? Perhaps the westbound Vikings were a tad tame by comparison.

Well, no. Not if you remember all the burning, battering, bashing and breaking-in the Vikings did when they ventured west to Britain and Ireland.

The western Vikings also got up to no good when they sailed down to France and invaded in the ninth century. Using rivers as highways for their longboats, the Vikings explored the country – and raided it. Churches were looted, houses were burned and people were terrorised.

These Vikings even set their sights as far south as the Mediterranean and North Africa.

In one celebrated episode from the year 859, a Danish leader called Hastein helped to lead a fleet of Viking ships through the Strait of Gibraltar. The Vikings attacked Spain, Morocco and southeast France before launching a cunning raid on the Italian city of Luna in 860.

Upon arrival at the city gates, Hastein pretended to be dead so that his men would be allowed to carry his coffin inside for a Christian burial. Once the Vikings had entered the town, however, Hastein leapt out of the coffin and drew his sword.

This was the signal for his men to pull out their own blades, which they had kept hidden under their robes. The Vikings wasted no time in slaughtering the citizens and ransacking the place.

Another infamous Viking raid took place in Paris in 885, although this time things didn't go according to plan.

Seven hundred longships and an army of 30,000 Viking warriors sailed up the River Seine and laid siege to the historic city, which was built on an island in the river. Longships were set on fire and rammed at a fortified bridge where soldiers were gathered to defend the city, but the Vikings were unable to break through in large numbers. When one Viking warrior was struck dead after entering a sacred tomb in the city, the Parisians believed God was helping them against the pagan invaders.

Eventually, an army of French reinforcements turned up. The Vikings agreed to leave provided they were paid off in treasure.

In 911, Paris was invaded again by a Viking pirate called Rollo. Although Rollo was fought off, the French king – whose name was Charles the Simple – knew that Rollo and the other Vikings would keep coming back to cause trouble. So a deal was struck.

Charles lived up to his name and kept the deal simple. On the condition that they stopped harassing French territory, the Vikings would get a patch of their very own to settle on. Can you guess what it was called?

A NORMANDY B VIKINGY C THINGY

The answer is [A]. The place was called Normandy on account of the fact that the Vikings were men from the north. So any Viking who settled there was a Norman – a 'North man'.

These were the same Normans who later conquered England. In fact, they had a massive impact on the whole of Europe, although they did become a lot more French and much less Viking once they settled down.

But enough about settlers. Let's get back to explorers.

It's time to meet the all-time greatest Viking adventurers. These were the ones who boldly went where no Viking (and probably no other European) had been before. To the edge of the world and beyond!

We're talking about the Vikings who sailed west across the North Atlantic to Iceland, Greenland and America – hundreds of years before the celebrated Atlantic voyage of Christopher Columbus.

The most famous of these Viking explorers were probably:

NADDOD | ERIK THE RED | LEIF ERIKSON

Let's begin with Naddodd. He was a Norwegian Viking who is said to have set sail west across the North Atlantic around the year 860. According to some reports, Naddodd was on his way to the Faroe Islands but got lost.

The story goes that Naddodd drifted across the sea until he came to the eastern shore of a strange new land. He climbed a mountain and looked out to see if he could see smoke rising from chimneys, or any other signs of human life. But there was none.

So he got back in his boat and set a course for the Faroe Islands again. But before he left, it began to snow.

It seems that Naddodd was not the only Viking to sail to Iceland around this time. A Swedish Viking called Gardar Svavarsson apparently ended up there after his mum told him to sail to the Scottish Hebrides and he got blown off course. And a Dane called Floki Vilgerdarson was allegedly guided to the remote island by a bird he set free from a cage.

A distant relative of Naddodd was Erik the Red. Erik was born in Norway some time around 951. When he was a boy, his dad killed a man and the family had to leave Norway.

They set off for Iceland, where Erik lived until he unwisely followed in his dad's footsteps. He also killed someone and was told to leave.

Erik sailed west to a new land, which he and his followers explored. It was a very cold and harsh place to live, and some earlier Viking visitors were said to have died there.

In order to impress people back in Iceland, Erik decided to give the new place a name that sounded like paradise. He called it 'Greenland'.

Erik reckoned the name would get people queuing up to settle there. He was right. Twenty-five ships set sail from Iceland, full of settlers, although only fourteen of them made it safely across the treacherous icy sea.

Erik the Red had three sons and one of them grew up to become a famous explorer too. His name was Leif Erikson.

Leif left his dad's colony on Greenland and sailed back to Norway, where he became a courtier of King Olaf I. Olaf persuaded Leif to give up his pagan ways and became a Christian.

Olaf wanted Leif to go back to Greenland and convert the people there to Christianity, too. So Leif set sail in about the year 1000. According to some reports, however, he was blown off course and got lost.

After a long ocean journey, Leif finally arrived at a new land. It was a beautiful place full of forests with trees that were perfect for building and grapes ideal for making wine.

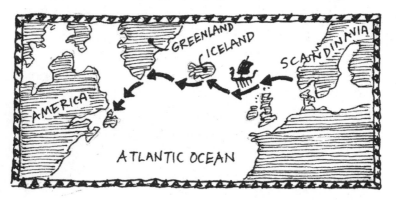

Leif gave the new land a name, which was Vinland. It was part of the continent we now call North America. Can you guess what 'Vinland' means?

A Land of forests
B Land of wine
C Land of lost Vikings

Well, Leif was more interested in wine than wood so the answer is B. After a while Leif left Vinland and went back across the ocean to continue his journey to Greenland.

When Leif finally got there he persuaded many Greenlanders to become Christians. These included his mum, who was so keen she had a Christian church built – the first one in Greenland.

There's another version of Leif's story, too. According to this version, before Leif left Norway he met a man called Bjarni Herjólfsson.

Bjarni, it turned out, had actually sailed to North America first – but he had not set foot on land. Bjarni gave Leif advice about how to reach America and sold him his boat.

Leif got together a crew of thirty-five men and put to sea. They eventually reached the undiscovered country of North America as planned.

Whichever version of Leif's story is true, there's one important thing to keep in mind. The Vikings were probably (although we can't be certain) the first Europeans to discover both Greenland and America – but they were certainly not the first people to live there.

That's because the native people of Greenland and North America were already living there. At different points in the history of Greenland, for example, these local groups or tribes of people included the Dorset, Thule and Inuit (the proper name for Eskimos).

For about four or five hundred years, Viking settlers lived alongside the Inuit on Greenland – although it seems the two tribes didn't mix much. In fact, some reports say they had the odd battle, with the Inuit using walrus teeth as weapons.

Eventually the Vikings disappeared from Greenland but no one knows exactly why. It might be because they never learned how to hunt and fish the local wildlife as well as the Inuit, so they eventually ran out of food and starved.

The Viking explorers' achievement was still massive, though. Few if any Europeans at that time had dared to sail so far west across the Atlantic and live to tell the tale.

After all that exploring, there was only one place a Viking had left to go. Was it:

A Outer Space?
B Valhalla?
C The bottom of the ocean?

Let's find out . . .

6

The Viking universe

Viking warriors hoped that when they died they would make the ultimate journey to Valhalla – the Viking heaven. Valhalla was part of a magical universe, and the Vikings believed that this universe surrounded the everyday world they lived in.

The Viking universe was divided up into different worlds, or realms. Nobody knows for sure what the realms were supposed to look like, or how they were organised. So the picture we have is sketchy. But we do know there was a rough total of Nine Realms.

The Nine Realms were connected to each other by a huge tree called Yggdrasil. Messages could be sent up and down the tree using a special message-carrying service. Can you guess what it was?

Believe it or not, the answer is C. The squirrel carried messages between an eagle at the top of the tree and a dragon called Nidhogg, which gnawed at its roots.

Except that the squirrel's name wasn't actually Dave. It was Ratatosk – which means 'drill-tooth'.

Perched in the tree's upper branches (some reports say its topmost roots) were three of the Nine Realms. These upper realms were called Vanaheim, Alfheim and Asgard. Inside Asgard was Valhalla.

In the middle of the tree (or its roots) were three more realms – Nidavellir, Jotunheim and Midgard. These middle realms were also connected to the upper level by a rainbow bridge known as Bifrost.

At the bottom of the tree, deep in its roots, were the realms of Muspelheim, Niflheim and Hel. As you can probably guess, Hel and the other lower realms were pretty nasty places. We'll go down to Hel later in this chapter – but don't worry, we won't hang about.

First, let's take a closer look at the upper realms. Among these, Asgard stood out as the highest of all. It contained stunning castles and fortresses, and was protected by a huge wall.

Asgard was the home of the Aesir, a group of warrior gods. The ruler of the Aesir was called Odin, and he was the most powerful of all Viking gods.

Odin is often thought of as tall and strong, with long hair and a beard. According to some reports he wore chainmail under his dark cloak and on his head a wide-brimmed hat. He rode an eight-legged horse called Sleipnir.

Perched on Odin's shoulders were two ravens called

Thought and Memory, and in his hand was a magical spear called Gungnir. When thrown, Gungnir never missed its target and always flew back into Odin's hand afterwards.

Odin had only one eye. The left one was poked out after he travelled to one of the roots of Yggdrasil in search of the well of knowledge.

The well was guarded by a giant called Mimir. The giant agreed to let Odin take a drink from the well in return for one of his eyes.

Mimir scooped up some of the sacred water in his horn and gave it to Odin to drink. When Odin did so, he suddenly felt very wise. Odin then gouged out his eye as agreed, and it was dropped in the well.

Odin was married to another very powerful god called Freya. Some reports say his wife was actually called Frigga, but Freya and Frigga were probably one and the same.

Freya was the god of beauty, love and art. She had some immense magical powers, such as an ability to see the future, and had a cloak made of feathers that allowed her to turn into a falcon and fly. Freya was also believed by some to be stepmother to Thor, the most famous of Odin's sons.

Thor was the guardian of Asgard. His main weapon was a hammer, and whenever he brought it crashing down on one of his enemies it caused thunder and lightning.

Inside Asgard was the Viking heaven of Valhalla, which means 'hall of the slain'. Valhalla was Odin's castle and its enormous great hall had 540 doors. This is where dying Viking warriors were brought by the Valkyries, who were Odin's warrior daughters.

When dead warriors arrived at Valhalla they didn't just sit around drinking, feasting and having a good time (although there was a lot of that). Odin told them to prepare for Ragnarok – the end of the world – when they would have to do battle with an army of giants and demons.

According to some reports, half of all the dead warriors actually went to a different place called Folkvang. This was a meadow in Asgard that belonged to Freya. If a warrior was unhappy about ending up in Folkvang instead of Valhalla, there doesn't seem to have been much they could do about it.

Next to Asgard were the realms of Alfheim and Vanaheim. Not much is known about these lands. Alfheim was the home of wondrous supernatural creatures called Light Elves. Vanaheim was a beautiful wilderness of forests and rivers, home to a group of gods called the Vanir.

The most important of the middle realms was Midgard – which means 'Middle Earth'. This is the everyday world where mortal humans lived.

The Vikings believed Middle Earth was surrounded by a never-ending and bottomless ocean that was impossible to sail across. In the ocean lived an enormous serpent called Jormungand, whose body was so long it circled around the whole world.

Near Middle Earth were the realms of Jotunheim and Nidavellir. Jotunheim was a freezing cold wasteland, home to terrifying giants whose capital city of Utgard was made of ice. Jotunheim was also home to Mimir's Well, where Odin lost his eye.

Nidavellir was the underground home of the dwarves. In a huge labyrinth of tunnels, mineshafts and workshops, the dwarves made magical tools and weapons of gold, iron and wood. These objects included Thor's hammer and Odin's spear.

The dwarves also made a magical ring, which could copy

itself to make more rings. They even made a longship that could be folded up and put in its owner's pocket.

Lower down still were the underworlds of Muspelheim, Niflheim and Hel. If you think some of the realms we have looked at so far sound strange, these are even stranger and very scary.

Muspelheim was a burning-hot realm, home to fire demons that were ruled over by a giant called Surt. Vikings believed that the sun and stars were created by sparks from Muspelheim.

Niflheim was a place of darkness and frozen mists, where the dead went if they didn't make it up to Valhalla. And even worse than that was Hel, which was said by some to be a realm inside Niflheim separated by a great wall and ruled by a goddess who was also called Hel. In Hel, the dragon Nidhogg gnawed at the corpses of the dead and drank their blood.

There might have been a tenth realm, too. This was Svartalfheim, which means 'Home of the Dark Elves'. The Dark Elves were nightmarish creatures which turned to stone if they went out into the sunlight.

Speaking of nightmares, that brings us back to Ragnarok – the end of the world. The word Ragnarok means 'twilight of the gods'.

The Vikings believed that Ragnarok took place when there was a great battle between the forces of good and evil. Leading the good side was Odin, who was joined by the gods of Asgard and the warriors of Valhalla.

The forces of evil were led by a mischievous god called Loki, who was Hel's father. Among his followers were the giants of Jotunheim, who sailed to the battlefield on a longship made of dead men's fingernails.

Loki's forces also included the fire demons of Muspelheim. The terrible giant Surt carried a flaming sword and threw huge fireballs that set the world aflame, while the battle between the two sides caused the great tree of Yggdrasil to catch fire and shake violently.

Almost all the gods, warriors and demons that fought in Ragnarok were destroyed. Odin grappled with a monstrous wolf called Fenrir, whose jaws were so huge they stretched from one end of the universe to the other and swallowed Odin up.

Thor wrestled with the great sea serpent, Jormungand. During the fight Thor managed to kill the beast, but not before he was bitten by it. He died soon afterwards from its poisonous venom.

Finally, with the world set on fire by Surt and most of the gods, monsters and heroes dead, the Nine Realms crumbled into the boiling ocean. The sun, the moon and the stars were all extinguished during the battle, and the universe was plunged into darkness.

Luckily, Ragnarok was not in fact the end of everything. From the ashes of the old world, a new world began to appear.

It turned out that Yggdrasil was not completely destroyed. From it there appeared two new humans – a woman and a man called Lif and Lifthrasir. Green shoots meanwhile began to grow by the light of a new sun. In this way, life returned to Middle Earth.

Some of the gods had also survived. In the upper realms they built new castles, peacefully played chess and told sad stories about the loss of their friends.

Down in the underworld, the demons rebuilt too. The dragon Nidhogg reappeared to gnaw on the flesh of the sinful dead and drink their blood.

If all this talk of flesh-eating dragons and calamitous battles between good and evil sounds scary, don't worry. Apart from the bit where humans lived, Middle Earth, the Viking universe was not real. Neither were its gods or demons.

What matters is that Vikings themselves believed in these things, so that means they were real in a way. They are definitely a very important part of Viking history.

In the next chapter, we'll take a look at some things people have suggested about the Vikings that even the Vikings themselves would have said were rubbish. Such as:

[A] The Vikings wore horned helmets
[B] They explored outer space
[C] Boys could be Vikings but not girls
[D] The Vikings fought in the Second World War
[E] They played American football

If you think some of these are just jokes, think again . . .

7

The curse of the horned helmet

By the end of the thirteenth century, the Viking age was over. Instead of all that raiding and land-grabbing the Vikings had mostly settled down and basically stopped being Vikings.

This does not mean, however, that the Vikings became extinct. In other words, they did not die out completely. Actual extinct things include:

Dinosaurs
Neanderthals
Betamax video cassettes

While we're at it, here's some things that probably *should* be extinct but unfortunately are not:

CHRISTMAS JUMPERS   HOMEWORK   BAD BREATH

But back to the Vikings. Instead of dying out, the Vikings simply changed their ways and became more modern.

On the other hand, many people would argue that the Vikings did not change completely. Some would even say that a sort of Viking way of life is still going strong.

For example, the Viking history you are reading about in the book still inspires people. Modern sailboats are often compared to Viking boats. Parliaments, where leaders meet to vote on important matters, are often compared to the old Viking meetings called *things*.

Tourists flock to historical Viking attractions, such as York, or Jorvik, in England, while many people enjoy taking part in Viking historical societies. Some even dress up and live like Vikings during their spare time.

At Lerwick in Shetland, a winter festival is held every year called Up Helly Aa. Islanders dress up like Vikings and take part in a torch-lit procession before setting fire to a Viking-style galley. The festival began in the nineteenth century and is still going strong.

Modern sportspeople are still compared to Viking warriors for their bravery or skill. And when someone gets really mad, people often say they have gone 'berserk' like a Viking.

The Vikings also inspire people with their myths and legends. Let's quickly remind ourselves what myths and legends actually are, because they are not quite the same thing as history.

Myths are made-up stories that people believe in, which can make them very important even though they are not real. Legends are usually a blend of fact and myth, which means a mixture of real bits and made-up bits.

Now, here's an important thing. There are two different kinds of Viking myths and legends:

1. Old Viking myths and legends.
2. New Viking myths and legends.

So let's think about what that means. First, we have the old Viking myths and legends. Old Viking myths include all the stuff you've learned about the Viking gods, the great tree of Yggdrasil and the giant squirrel called Dave. No wait, sorry – the squirrel called Ratatosk.

Those myths, or beliefs, were at the heart of the Vikings' pagan religion.

The Vikings were keen on legends, too. Take the story of Ragnar Lodbrok, for example. He is said to have been a heroic Danish king who lived in the ninth century.

Ragnar's surname Lodbrok meant 'leather breeches'. He is reputed to have raided Paris and battled the Anglo-Saxons before being captured and thrown in a snake pit to die.

However, the stories about Ragnar are actually legends. In fact, some modern historians say he never existed at all.

A lot of what we know about Viking myths and legends (and facts) comes from books written by medieval Viking historians. One of the most famous was Snorri Sturluson, who lived in Iceland in the twelfth and thirteenth centuries.

Besides being a historian, Snorri had also been a poet. The Viking word for a poet was *skald*. The *skalds* wrote long poems, which they read out or sang for the entertainment of Viking nobles and kings.

The poems were about lots of things – romance, jokes, arguments, myths and history. An evening of poetry would often also include songs and music played on Viking instruments such as the Lur – a cone-shaped wooden horn.

By Snorri's time, not only had the old Viking way of life pretty much disappeared, but the Vikings had also changed their religion to Christianity. Though many still believed in the old pagan gods like Odin, the Christian God was now more important.

Something else was changing too, and that's where the new Viking myths and legends come in. As the centuries went by, people began making up new stories about the Vikings.

Some of these stories are legends with a grain of truth to them, but some are just false myths. Let's take a look . . .

TRUE OR FALSE?
Vikings only visited people to split their skulls and steal their treasure.

You know from what you have read here that many Vikings actually preferred peaceful trading. They only nicked stuff and flattened folk if they absolutely had to. Although, to be fair, that happened quite often. **Verdict: FALSE**

Vikings were all scruffy, uncivilised barbarians.

In fact, you know that the Vikings often wore beautiful clothes and jewellery, played clever games like chess and built sophisticated boats and houses. Mind you, when they *did* split people's skulls it must have made their clothes pretty scruffy.

Verdict: FALSE

Vikings sacrificed humans.

According to some reports, the Vikings carried out two types of human sacrifice. The first went like this: when an important Viking died, a thrall – a slave – could be killed and buried along with him. The second was when a human was sacrificed to please Odin or some other god.

Verdict: TRUE

Boys could be Vikings but not girls.

There were loads of women around during Viking times, of course, but the important fact is that some were into classic Viking things like thieving, exploring or making mincemeat out of their enemies. Two tough Viking women of this kind were Ragnhild of Orkney and Aud the Deep-Minded.

Ragnhild, who lived in the tenth century, was the daughter of Erik Bloodaxe. She was married a few times and plotted the murder of three of her husbands.

I couldn't stand the way he chewed his food!

Aud the Deep-Minded was the wife of Olaf the White. After her husband was killed in Ireland, she moved to Scotland, then sailed to Iceland. She became one of the first Viking settlers there.

Verdict: FALSE

We can learn about the Vikings from comic strips and films.

Since the 1950s there have been many comics and films about the Vikings and their gods, such as Thor. The exciting stories in comics and films are mostly made up, or fictional, but they can give you some basic ideas about Vikings. Then you can check the facts in a good book or website about Viking history.

Verdict: TRUE

Only people with red or blond hair can have Viking ancestors.

Some Vikings had light hair, but plenty of others had dark hair. So lots of different modern people can have Viking ancestry, not just blond ones.

DNA tests have shown that many modern people from the Scottish isles of Orkney, Shetland and the Hebrides have Viking ancestors. Several mainland Scottish clans also claim descent from Vikings, as do some families in England and Ireland.

Verdict: FALSE

Many of our modern ideas about the Vikings were cooked up during the nineteenth century. During that time, writers, musicians and artists became really interested in the Vikings. Two of the most famous were:

Sir Walter Scott – a best-selling Scottish novelist and poet, whose writing was inspired by Viking history and myth.

Richard Wagner – a celebrated German composer, who wrote an opera series inspired by the Vikings called *The Ring of the Nibelung.*

Thanks to writers, composers and artists there was a 'Viking craze' in the 1800s. People just couldn't get enough of all things Viking.

With perfect timing, a hoard of Viking treasure was discovered in a sand dune after a storm in the Western Isles of Scotland around 1831. This treasure was a collection of small figurines now known as the Lewis Chessmen.

Since then, interest in the Vikings has never really gone away. During the Second World War, for example, some armies liked to compare themselves to elite Viking warriors.

Between the 1930s and 1950s, Viking history and myths helped inspire a historian called JRR Tolkien to write a series of famous fantasy novels called *The Hobbit* and *The Lord of the Rings*. Tolkien's fictional stories are set in a place called 'Middle Earth' and feature dwarves, fire demons and lots of other things from Viking culture.

In more recent times there has been no end to the list of things inspired by the Vikings. These include:

Viking spacecraft – Back in 1975 two space probes called *Viking 1* and *Viking 2* were launched and put on a course for the planet Mars. The probes' names

were inspired by the bold explorers of Viking history. They reached their destination a year later and sent back invaluable information about the red planet.

Viking sports teams – The Minnesota Vikings are an American football team, and just one of many teams in different sports that have been inspired by the historical Vikings' toughness and teamwork.

Viking pop music – The word Viking has popped up on guitars, drum kits, song lyrics, albums, you name it . . . And many rock bands have dressed up like Vikings while wielding their guitars like battle-axes and making a thunderous racket that Thor would be proud of.

Viking shopping – You can buy all sorts of things these days with the word 'Viking' on them. These are usually products that want to appear strong and sturdy. Examples include car tyres, pens, lawn mowers, sticky tape, cookers, life rafts, and lots more.

We also use a lot of Viking words in our everyday conversations. Jarls, karls and thralls are just three of the many Viking – or Old Norse – words you have already picked up in this book. Here are some other English and Scots words that have been handed down to us by the Vikings:

BAIRN – another word for child

BRIG – this means bridge

CAKE – comes from Old Norse word kaka

GUN – from the girl's name Gun or Gunilda, meaning 'battle'

KIRK – another word for church

KNIFE – is almost the same as Old Norse word knifr

THURSDAY – named after the god THOR, as in Thor's day

WINDOW or WINDAE – from the word vindauga, which means 'wind's eye'

But wait. We began this chapter by talking about Viking myths – and we almost forgot about the biggest myth of all. The horned helmet!

In the nineteenth century it became fashionable to think of Viking warriors as having worn helmets with animal horns stuck on them. Modern historians say this is false, and the horned helmet gives people the wrong impression of what the Vikings were really like.

In fact, historians and archaeologists insist that Vikings wore cone-shaped helmets with no horns. Yet people still dress up like Vikings by wearing plastic horned helmets. It's a sort of curse.

For now we can categorically, and one-hundred-per-cent definitely say, the Vikings NEVER wore any horned helmets. That's until someone goes and digs one up, of course!

Timeline

750 AD	Vikings travel to Russia and other lands around this time or earlier.
789	The first recorded Viking attack on England takes place.
793	Lindisfarne monastery is raided and burned by Vikings.
795	The Scottish island of Iona is raided, then attacked again in 802 and 806.
841	After raiding Ireland for decades, the Vikings conquer Dublin.
856	Rhodri Mawr defeats Viking invaders in Wales.
859	A fleet of Viking ships attacks Morocco in North Africa.
860	A Viking sailor called Naddodd discovers Iceland.
866	A great Viking army invades England and later establishes the Danelaw.
870	Vikings destroy the Celtic fortress at Dumbarton Rock in Scotland.

911	Vikings permitted to settle in Normandy after harassing France for decades.
982	Explorer Erik the Red arrives in Greenland.
1000	Leif Erikson discovers Vinland (North America).
1014	Vikings defeated at the Battle of Clontarf in Ireland.
1016	Knut the Great becomes King of England.
1066	Vikings defeated in England at the Battle of Stamford Bridge.
1179	Birth of Viking poet and historian Snorri Sturluson in Iceland.
1263	Vikings defeated in Scotland at the Battle of Largs.
1468–1469	Norway gives the islands of Orkney and Shetland to Scotland.